BLACK SEEDS

THE POETRY AND REFLECTIONS OF TARIQ TOURÉ

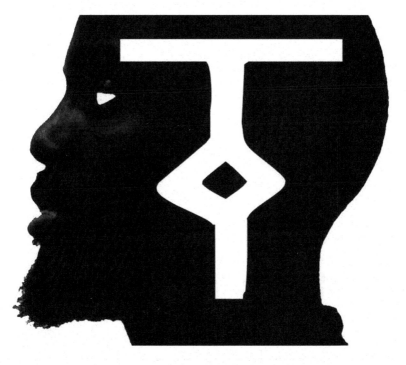

PHOTOS BY KYLE POMPEY AND SHANNON WALLACE

zerflin
did the design

INTRODUCTION

This book was born out of the dark vestiges and radiant light that is the American ghetto. This book was chiseled out of the redemptive power of the Black University. Black art, as it manifests itself throughout our lifetimes, has been beyond mere coping mechanisms and spiritual exercise.

Our expression embodies our intrinsic power to move anything made up of atoms. I pray you approach the following prose and illustrations with an open soul, and warmed heart.

Love will free us.
Art will light the path.

"The word "art" is something
the West has never understood"

—Amiri Baraka

For my two lights.

I know children
Who dream of running
Across acres stretched forth
As far as the eyes can see
With vegetation tilled
By promises their ancestors kept
Sacrifices their Ancestors held to with their teeth

I know children
Who love truth more than caramels
That spend Saturdays
Spinning like tops in the middle of living rooms
That never made room for living

I know children
Whose only wishes
Are to strut as lions do
Sing as birds sing
Fly as Swann fly
Howl as Wolves howl
But for all their ambitions
They encounter bullets
And die as warriors die
For being

Chicago

you. remind me. of my. grandmas. porch
cousins. that. doubled. as. sisters
house. parties. where. anything. could happen.

but we happened.

where 5 ft. tall. black boys. wore pistols. like underwear.
corner-store. trips. that. stretched. 2 dollars into. 20
of girls named. Shawntay. that. channelled the Euphrates

in. their. bouyant hips.

of collard greens. yams. and embattled. english.
but. i. am. sure that. the window. i am. peering. through.
is. completely. different for. someone else.

Nomad Yard

Prayer
without works
is like
the well intentioned
laborer who
embarks on the task
of excavating
all the world's beaches
scooping
the fine grains
of sand
with a spoon

"Sabr"

Have you not seen the woman who bends gravity?
And carries the universe in her left pocket?
She who stares through the souls of men?
Have you not seen the woman of brick and butterflies?
    she who speaks in Sun Rays?
    I have bore witness
    to your ruby encrusted ambition
    I have wished to speak sweetnesses
    in your presence
    and uttered murmurs
    tripped by the palpitations of a heart
too vulnerable for your journey
You are the morning wind to a lost ship
Lighthouse for the blind
God took time with you...
Pouring his essence in ounces at a time...
And we are left to chase the drops from his chalice.

For Black Girls who Fight

Be bold
At times the shy don't shine
When the brave don't speak the weak don't mind
Humble mumbles in the dark are lost in time
Is he who flies not better than the one who climbs?
Is he who shimmers better than he who blinds?
Is he who searches better than he who finds?
I surmise my pity in our cowardice demise
Shame scurries when you roar

> Fear buckles when you bark
> Courage kicks down doors
> Doubt deepens the dark
> Pride hidden is prison that

Weakens the part
Shout from your chest
Speak from your heart
Because until then no one knows you

Screams of Courage

South
Baltimore Harbor
Tunnel Thruway
REDUCED
VISIBILITY

curled up in shards of lost hopes and ambitions
I write and rip away my assumptions
about this abysmal existence called life
eyes heavy as 100% Columbian cocaine feels strapped to
mules going through customs
my limbs sway like hair on my
6 year old nieces angelic face
                        this is me fighting the poet
                        that lives inside my poetry
                        he haunts me, he is the reason
                        I write in witty soliloquy
                        he is the knots in my stomach
he cares nothing about my semantics
even less about my rapture
he sits at an old mission style desk
eyes glazed over red as Monroe's devilish lips,
peering through reading glasses,
unmoved

Writer's Block I

19

We are more than boogaloo tunes and pulsating 808s
The jungle music in our feet rumbles
from cuticles to esophagus
Drenched in sweat we twist, turn,
burn holes in the flo, Hell yeah
Hair flies round lashing the air, as we dip low
Low like the black of the ocean
Low like roads railed to railroad bondage
We lift ancestors to their feet, roots above the trees
We are the music that bring nations to their knees
We are the elephant in the room
We are the drum
Beat
    Breaking
        Silence
           And
              Sound Barriers when we feel like it

More

I
called
your
momma
yesterday
she
took
your
side

0 – 35

Through my Travels I find faces

Faces that told stories mouths couldn't mouth

Faces that held secrets that dare not be shared

Faces filled with scarves that covered scars

Faces that made ponds filled with tears of joy

      Faces that demanded a chance

      Faces that knew simply wishing wasn't enough

Faces that sometimes told too much

Faces that were the last human thing to hold on to

Faces that said everything without talking

Faces that never grew old

As for me, I can never forget a face

Masks

it was expected for us die here
be it the lead bullet
or lead paint
we endured
on hope and Ramen

every awakening reassured
the Lords favor on us
the supposed commodities
of Reaganomics
who resisted
the summons Of apathy

delivering blows to Moynihan
when the cameras came
you found a small village fighting
when the cameras left
you found a small nation surviving
our renaissance is right on time

North & Pennsylvania

Find yourself in realms of uncertainty where maybe...
Everyone has jewels wrapped in knives &...
A pond awaits subconsciously that...
Ripples with every pebble dropped in imagination...

No mistake here
Only divine decree

Mostly
All of us
Need to listen to silence's symphony and command

False Expectations Appearing Real

Paint me a broken winged angel

Paint me a square off angle

Paint me a wishing well without a coin inside

Paint me an ocean coast without a tide

Paint me suffocated no wind to suckle

Paint me mischievous en route to trouble

Paint me bruised beaten, obsolete

Paint me defeated, cowering, in retreat

Paint me stumped, ignorant, oblivious

Paint me lazy distraught, insidious

Paint me cast off forever by the crowd

Paint me homeless beaten by brows

Paint me spineless unable to endure

Paint me stumbling towards death's corridor

Paint me in misery humbled by my past

And if you should paint me first,

Make sure to paint me last

6:13AM

I was a genius once
It was 1988
at 6:13PM
I had just been born
Man...
what a moment

Tabula rasa

"Good Morning Class today is career day,
but before I bring in our first guest speaker
I'd Like to ask you all a question:
What do want to be when you grow up?"

India jumped up and instantly proclaimed
"I wanna be a College Professor"
And Stews hand shot in the air with the speed of light
And he said "I'm gonna be a Firefighter"
Little ole couldn't Kevin couldn't help himself so he yelled
"I'm gonna be an NBA Allstar"
From the left of the class
came the sweet voice of Lia saying
"Ms Johnson, I wanna Be a Doctor"
Brianna came alllll the way to the front of the class
and said "I'm gonna be an astronaut"

And a little hand rose from way
deep in the back of the class
And Ms. Johnson face turned up with a frown
And she knew she had to ask
"What do u wanna be Jamal?"
And Jamal stood tall like he couldn't hold it all
But he decide to take a stand
He said "Ms.. Johnson I just... wanna be a black man"
And Ms. Johnson said, "whoa whoa whoa Jamal
Do you know with that means?"
Jamal said "yup."
"There's some lines that I won't walk between"
Like the lines that say I'll have to settle for less
Or let you diagnose my intelligence
With their standardized test

It'll mean that sometimes I'll probably have to read
Because there's some things in history
That I'll probably need
To know
Because if I'm Ignorant
I'll be another old wino sayin 'come here youngin
Lemme tell u bout life'
All drunk and belligerent

But to me Ms. Johnson I think it's pretty easy
Like if I make the decision to make a baby
There can't be no leaving
And I'll have to hold the little sucker
If it's colicky because it's teething
And to be a Blackman is to be the best specimen alive
Because it seems to me that we'd rather be
Anything but who we are deep inside
I'll have to refuse to sell my dignity for a pimped out ride
Because doing a Jig on BET is the equivalent
To me of serving fries
A Black man has to stand up for our rights
And fight for Job equity laws
And understand that the way out or our pay route
Doesn't rely on running or shooting a ball
Because sheesh, I ain't got to be Shaq
Just because I'm getting tall
I wonder what Shaka Zulu would say if
All our war generals were Coaching football
I'll have to remember what went on in states like Alabama
And then I'd understand that most of the B.S.
On the top 10 countdown is false propaganda
Because I refuse to be Lynched by your Old World Order
Can't pay attention to anything that them text taught us

Because
        Page 1 says
"Be University student don't try to create one"
        Page 2 says
"If you need money find a guy with
Skin like yours and take some"
        Page 3 says
"Jordans are more important than a college education"
        Page 4 says
"You can't support your family without an illegal occupation"
        Page 5 says
"Come on meet all your buddies down at the police station"
        Page 6 says
"You shouldn't set yourself limits
But we want you to put limits on your limitations"
        Page 7 says
"Why show all this love when you can all do some hating?"
        Page 8 says
"Take all of these, drugs, media, and sports
And use it for sedation"
        Page 9 says
"You're allowed to focus on what really matters on
occasion"
        Page 10 says
"If we can complete steps 1 through 10
You'll help us enslave nations"

But them trying to force me to say
I can't is what I can't stand
Because I'll have to believe I can
If I am gonna be a Black man...
Class dismissed

Black Seeds

Penny Pinching Politicians
Push Promises Preying
Pastors Praying Purveying
Pain Profiting Proposing
Problems Producing Profit
Prophet Pariahs Progeny
Planning Persecution Permeating
Prominent Personas People

PLEASE

Keep your ballot and the box it came in

Message to Grassroots

alleys blanketed by the wingspan of dusk
no longer shriek at me
the boroughs of my heart like the alley have witnessed the
failed parrying of my whims amongst seclusion
I'm a loser who has never tasted defeat
and I have sobbed in solace
the brick and mortar has fell
from my acidic dimensions

I am perpetrator and witness
of my own felonies
a life amidst the shadows
cannot be identified as life
it is an alley
                a mere means for travelers
                to ration ticks from time pieces
                where sailors dispose of fallen relics
                vegetation rarely emerges through
                the crevices of the boroughs
                in which I dwell

apart of everything while remaining nothing

Writer's Block II

Ego, like a rabid dog
Must be taken
Wayyyy out in the pasture
And put to sleep

But instead,
Men have cradled it
As Moses was cradled
Men have nurtured it
As Moses was nurtured
Men have loved it
As Moses was loved

Thus turning themselves
Into little Pharoahs

Atoms, Atom, Adam

I got a Way with words,
meaning—I got away with words,
I'm from where white birds sling
caged birds sing,
And you too, can smell fumes,
from hell rooms,
where they do the interrogating

Fugitive of The Ghetto

my mother asks why we spend so much time on the phone
yesterday morning i almost made a mistake and told her
that lately your stepfather has been trying to mold
you into man by wrapping his knuckles around your
temple and left jawbone, you said he hits like BITCH
and your mom played ring girl for the 3rd night in a row I
almost made the mistake of letting her know that
you left during the middle of the night
last week and slept at a place that you still haven't told me
about she does pay the bill on this phone and I think if she
knew that after football practice we walked in the mall
counting the marshmallow colored squares beneath
our feet with nothing but bus passes in our pockets but
common hopes and you told me while we sipped water
from the fountain that your father had an opportunity
to play ball professionally but he don't like to talk about
that, and that he ain't talked much at all because that
conversation happened 7 years ago and you ain't seen him,
but this is her phone technically so just call me tomorrow
around 10, she be sleep round that time and we can talk
more about the game

The Cost of Lending an Ear at 14 Years Old

I created
these words
while you
played
on my
lap

1st Born

Should you happen to be...
Covered in anything but
Paper white skin
Mourn Quickly
Bleed Quickly

Die

But by all means
Proclaim your forgiveness
From the mountaintops

Restrictions may Apply

I pray the love you find is like
A fistful of penny candies
Trapped lightning bugs in jars
Feet sunken in dew covered grass
No school on Monday
Ginger Tea
Awkward hugs
My Mommas cookin
Pitter Patter from young girls
Pounding concrete
Playing double dutch &...
Black boys fightin ova nickels

Cornerstore Folklore

guns drawn on fudge canvases
chalked Sidewalks
and nicknames we never forget

salmon Skies
same color as redbones named Diamond
that never got diamonds
who you mindin?

my ghetto be 4th of July on Tuesday
Baghdad on Thursday
Ghana on Friday
& Mississippi mo'nings on Sunday

I bought a 1 way ticket to someday
when bullets ain't bustin through family trees
we's got ta be Mo than alright

becuz Me,
fitna be free

21229

Starve 10 People in a room for 2 weeks
Place 60 inch TVs on all 4 walls in that same room
Play people on those TVs eating buffets,
Tossing chicken wings back and forth, sometimes
Throwing them in the garbage for fun
On the 14th day slide a steaming hot chicken dinner
In the middle of all 10 people
They rip each other to shreds for the meal
5 Lose their lives in the fight
Record the entire process
Leave the very end of the fight on 24 hour repeat
For everyone outside the room
Don't show the starvation, the marginalization
Only the very end of the carnage
Blame them for their animal like behavior
Explain that this is something unique to their kind
When one picks the lock and breaks out the room
Hold them in high standard
A symbol of excellence
Ask the remaining ones,
"Why can't you be just like that person?"
Tell them that if they could only be more "respectable"
They could survive
Rinse Repeat...

This is the ghetto

Redline

I daydreamed about a world with the absence of murder
Where lips were unable to tell lies

Cries

That came about because elation dug far inside
And burst in euphoria
Where scars from broken promises were a badge of honor
In this world children took candy from strangers
Perfection means you were a little stranger

Where helping hands

Are in such abundance
I didn't know which one to grab
Where funerals echo with laughs
And reality worth rejoicing over
and over
and over
again

Walking in Euphoria

as families cry out
and accusations are flung
children are lost
as the gavels are rung
the Prophets of our people
rush to the dung

Crisis Whores

Art should black eyes and bruise egos
Redeem the prostitute and shame the Preacher
Art should smell like mint tea and taste of epiphanies
Be a refuge for the virgin and prison for the pedophile
Art should quiet thunder and package lightning
Scream at the miser and comfort the vagabond
Yet I am lost, searching for what Art has in store for me

Conversations with myself, about myself.

I not only watched God mold you
Out of honey and orphaned stars
But poison tipped thorns
And fragrances that whispered
"Don't come any closer"
Still I curiously enjoy suckling
Pricked thumbs
Knowing
The outcomes of your embrace
I bathe in blissful
Drips
Of
Dopamine

Danger

Before our Ancestors filled the bottom of Earth's pools in passage
We knew our Black Life Mattered
Before Chains smothered the diaspora and labeled me a savage
We knew our Black Life Mattered
Before Cotton was King and Queens were captured
We knew our Black Life Mattered
Before Jim Crow restructured death and disaster
We knew our Black Life Mattered
Before Crack left neighborhoods scorched and scattered
We knew our Black Life Mattered
Before Mass incarceration turned babies into bastards
We knew our Black Life Mattered
Before Emmitt Till's body was beaten and battered
We knew our Black Life Mattered
Before Mike Brown was shot dead and humanity ravaged
We knew our Black Life Mattered
Before Rekia Boyd's hopes were torn and tattered
We knew our Black Life Mattered
Before Sandra Bland was robbed of a happily ever after
We knew our Black Life Mattered
Before Freddie Gray's spine broke and city was fractured
We knew our Black Life Mattered
Before a demon took the soul of 8 worshippers and a pastor
We knew our Black Life Mattered
Before we wait on souls to face judgement and rapture
You'll know our Black Life Mattered

BLM

Many will rage: Few will be patient
Many will cry out: Few will gather themselves
The Streets will flood with anger: Few will ORGANIZE

Entropy

a mother takes quivering steps
toward uncertainty
with hope & trauma resting in her saliva

a fetus rolls about in a womb
in divine security
with jubilance at the tips of its fingers

both are entering a "Mighty" land
where they will be hated
for needing love

Syria

Failure's supple kiss
Experiences napalm embrace of wisdom
The blessings of getting burned
How we fathom what really isn't
Trial & Error for every tumult there's a triumph
Crawling back from the grave is not happenstance
It's a science
The mountains of kings and decor of valleys of defeat
Impossible is hollow with the batter of belief
Silence the chatter of the teeth
Never put the sword in it sheath
Life is war
Until we're buried in the deep

Nothing

From the "boy you better nots!"
To the "put that downs!"
To my pops unfastening his belt making the click clack sound
From the bruised knees and busted lips
To "look a man in the eyes and keep a firm grip"
"Pull your pants up high boy"
"Don't sit in your seat slumped low"
Simple nuances that help a young man grow
I recollect these things in my childhood
Because I realize Lil Ty don't know

You see Ty is a kid from where the sun scared
To get shot if it shines too bright
From where female children raise children
While their children's father's grind at night
From where glances and gestures
Lead to militant advances and vests
And nike hoodies tied up tight
Ty sits on his stoop
A glimpse of the truth
That the body inhibiting his timberland boots
Is yet another kid some weak nigga ignored
See we'll sex u like man
By a meal if we can
But then we piss our pants
When it's time to raise a boy

For lil Ty as they call him
I wonder what life had in store
Mom will pick and choose different dudes
To beat her black and blue emotionally
And Ty will watch it all
But she doesn't understand remotely to see
That the container that is Ty's mind is being filled with experiences
That won't make him the man she hopes him to be

So the first thing that Ty learns concretely in his mind
Is to love her but, not to respect women
Shall we talk about Ty's decisions?

Now he'll figure those niggas who pour liquor
And twist swishas are the most qualified to play his father's role
And after about 2 years of drugging humping and slumming
Ty's heart turns cold

Equipped with a mean bop
His stare will make u lean akh
He keeps that .45 clean cocked
Boom! Put it to your nose
6 66's on his on his report card them white teach for america
teachers play devil's advocate
He'll learn geometry on them corners
How to subtract from hoodrats
And in that kitchen chemistry till he's mastered it
But you dunno half of it
All we see is a bastard kid
See in my line of work it's inevitable that me and Ty
Will have to have a sit
Down
And I'll have to pour him a tall glass of reality
And he'll have to have a sip

And I'll be like "Black boy you're only heightening the average"
"Of young black males makin it on the casket list"
Because making it out of high school is like a sweet 16
Look how deep the brackets is
If he don't grow to be 7 foot 5
Or can throw a ball a mile with the other civilized savages
He'll be labeled ADHD ADD PCP MP3 HDTV
And a host of other acronyms
So where's Ty's pot to piss in when the system's pissin in his in pot?

To Make it worst he's being uprooted from his block
Yuppies pay long dough for condos
So gentrifications thickening the plot

And we don't learn or be concerned
Until Ty goes missing or gets shot
Because
From the "boy you better nots!"
To the "put that downs!"
To my pops unfastening his belt making the click clack sound
From the bruised knees and busted lips
To "look a man in the eyes and keep a firm grip"
"Pull your pants up high boy"
"Don't sit in your seat slumped low"
Simple nuances that help a young man grow
I recollect these things in my childhood
Because I realize Lil Ty don't know

You see Ty is a kid from where the sun scared
To get shot if it shines too bright
From where female children raise children
While their children's father's grind at night
From where glances and gestures
Lead to militant advances and vests
And nike hoodies tied up tight
Ty sits on his stoop

Concrete Roses

I see empires in your furrowed eyebrows

Revolution in your swollen lips

Ancestors in your walk

God in your fists

Nubia

I sat down
to write a poem
got up
and put
the pieces
of ego
in a
brown bag
and
carried them away

Stop reading Lorde

Embrace the direction the ups and downs are taking you
Appreciate the way the bitter and sweet is shaping you
Beware of people who take energy away from you
Become who you are and there is no replacing you

What if your what if works?

I'm patient enough to wait
For you to love the things about me
That don't exude perfection
The things that only get spoken on
Under curious moonlight
On pea green grass
If we should both confess our sins
Let it be under the condition
That death will be only in tune
With our secrets

Open Lines of Communication

I think I'd rather try to cheat death than try to cheat love
because if I die then I'll finally get some sleep!!!

But uhhh, Love knows no slumber and it's no wonder when
ya meet her, she's Infinity and 0
and never experienced defeat

I like to think about her because
I know she's thinking about me,
even though at night she makes it hard to count the sheep

But I'd rather be an insomniac,
than to spend a minute without her
and I know I'm in too deep

My homies say "Huh, look brotha you caught up you need to
knock her her and her off and play it like a G"

And I could but that games old
I guess you can say I'm playin it like a B.

Well I guess I am, because this Beautiful Black Brother
can't Barely begin to Believe that these Broads
might Bring me the same Breath
taking experience that she gives me
where I can Barely even Breathe

You see

To never feel love is like being trapped in a cave all your life
only to one day finally be released

And when you walk out your eyes feel all types of pain
because she's like sunlight

Too much will make it hard for you to see.

My People

We're all standing on a Goldmine all we have to do is take the time to look beneath!

And I Promise she don't bite well she might, but that's besides the point I'm trying to get you to believe

The point is she don't give a damn about how much of rude boy your perceived to be

And hunnie understand that sellin me sex only makes you one more Halle Berry branch on a Divah tree

She's the first human emotion

So all I ask is that you embrace your originality

Whatever happen to candlelight dinners
or dancing in the street!

I just want you to feel how she makes me feel

Kind of like I'm flying, but I'm standing on my feet

But you know I'm gonna end this now

Because obviously I'm putting you poor excuses for humans gently to sleep

Ladies and gentleman boys and girls

"In the red corner weighing in at a whopping 1 trillion pounds standing sky high!

And the crowd says

Love

She cried
6 rivers
Over a Man-child
Too maladroit to know she was God

I'm still taking gulps
Trying to fill my heart
With water too shallow to tread
And yet too deep to stand in

She, Her, Sometimes

Stop searching for the Universe's
silent answers in hollowed people,
naturally the sound reverberates
through the halls of their jaws
due to emptiness of their hearts
corridors which contain nothing on nothing
we confuse volume for validation
mankind forfeits a poignant now
for pungent hallucination that
echoes over what needs to be
seen, heard, or said twice

Lectures to my Self-esteem

Man is given seconds, yet begs for minutes
Given minutes, yet begs for hours
Given hours, yet begs for days
Given days, yet begs for months
Given months, yet begs for years
Given years, yet begs for a lifetime
Given a lifetime, yet he has never halted himself
To praise the moment he exists in
Then he is given death...

Such is the life of human beings

The curious attention span

Paper contracts as the muscles do of an

Austrian gold medalist lifter

8.5 x 11 is transformed into the white canyon

I am running, escaping, through a desert with no boundaries

Life eclipsing with thirst.

The inability to navigate the silence of my evolution

Proves I am farther from existing and nearer to ceasing

A lead lance weighs heavy on my palm

A weapon for a mere mercenary

Impossible to determine whether I wield it or it wields me

Whispers lament viciously

"Strike with fury of a slave's revolt"

"Strike with the passion of an avenging lover"

Carve legend into the canyon

Run geometric patterns in the desert

Shout the tales of revolution into the silence

Leap to the moon

And split the sun

Writers Block III

They picked apart our peace and
Piled it in pieces
Made prostitutes out of my nephews
and deflowered all my nieces
I'm just a poor poet with too much pride not to preach it
Radio airwaves got me seasick
I vomit up an answer
2 more rump shaking songs on the top 10 countdown
Add 2 more to the cancer
She laughs and giggles when they whistle
or a benz honks its horn
Developed curves in a summer now she wonders,
how to use them
Another world star is born
As the world starts to pour
It's libation called reality
I see my nephew on Facebook
showing off his abnormalities
Signs of final frontier of a future of fear
From father fueling fallacies

Martin died on a balcony
Malcolm died on stage
They were our best alchemist
How we supposed to get paid
Because everything that's gained and given
That glitters ain't guaranteed to be gold
They package the lives of dope fiends
and killed teens in sixteens
It's guaranteed to be sold
I manifest these rhymes while
Time manufactures the results
Blink twice at Youtube and you too
can have your child caught up in this cult

Strolling in the tenement getting cold stares
from my brethren
Extolling my sentiment when I climb those stairs
It better not be one damn ghetto up in heaven
Colleges say come get an education
to get off welfare and bid it farewell
But the 3 degrees I'm getting
ain't the 98 degrees in kitchens
Our kids still pitching in the stairwell

Wishful hoping praying and thinking about the day when
When black fathers kiss they daughters
And take hood pictures by their sons playpen
Instead in these caucuses these politicians
Circle our black carcasses as high priced vultures
Now combine a combine and the new slave auction
That's accepted in our culture

Play him offense and defense
that wont big nigger wont break
For them increments he tearing up ligaments
Shots of cortisone to the bone
that big nigga gonna play
Private school girl found floating around
All-Star weekend hallways
What they didn't understand is that
ignorance doesn't discriminate to class
And you don't really feel it
until little Dillon
starts "Project Xing" on his dad

They say look how far we come
Ain't you happy to see?
I say they gave us fancy boats
We still stranded at sea

The Fabric of Our Lives

77

they tell us
to pull up our pants
and it'll be ok.

i can't help
but Notice
the Black Men lynched
in 3 piece suits

from back in the day...

Respectable Genocide

i see Black men's gums...
teeth, plaque and tongue
shuckin & Jivin fa Sugar
from the Grandchildren of cotton
pin stripe suited
in wingtips that shine like harvest moons
tap dancin to twisted tunes
of progress and freedom
hope semantics Drip from their Saliva
but we know Sambo
been fixin to be just like Massa...
for a while now

Obmas

I have friends
Who sit & pontificate
Musing over Plans
To leave
More than
A biological imprint
7 generations
Down the stream
Where
Apple headed children
Trip over
Their forefathers & foremothers
Legacies
On the way to school

And

I have friends
That have only
Planned
For Saturday night

Balance

Come brother, Come from under the suspicious spell
of tokenized lies, demonic distortions of your past
that was never a jungle they found you in
there was never a people waiting to be civilized
your minds been run through the gauntlet
your thoughts been drenched in the ravine
find your armor today
find your armor today

Come sister, come from off that mountain
of expectations, poisonous portrayals
you everything they been praying on bein
you every sight they been waiting on seein
find a room to light up tonight
find a room to light up tonight

ain't no struggle without your grace
aint no struggle without your mercy
whole world spinning on your manicured finger
I'd be humbled whenever you decide
To make it stop on your command

101

I dare you to be unapologetically
Blacker than you've ever been
—Blacker than
"Gimme all my change back after you buy my Newports"
Blacker than corner boys in New Balances
Out of Balance in the land of obtuse dreams
Blacker than Potato salad
bursting through Reynolds wrap on Your 5th cookout
Blacker than getting every twistin motion right
To that new dance
because a party ain't a party
Until it's ran all through

I dare you
To overbook in this spades game because if not
We gotta wait 2 Fridays to redeem ourselves
Be unapologetic about them hot comb burns
Across yo fo'head
About yo cousin who in rehab
But had a jumpa sweeta than
Pistol pete
About the hand me down
Handed down
A lil too tight fo' comfort

I dare you
to lock in them pell grants
grant granny's wish
that you be the first one
to walk cross that stage
yea you
yea you
you be the first one
to walk cross that stage
walk cross that stage
walk cross that stage
but remember
what brought you here
don't
deserve
no
apologies
"Now where is my 2 dollas and fitty cent?"

Unapologetically Black

6 Street generals
Cemented in stances at arms distance.
All posturing smoothly
Shoulders slumped low
Cascading towards concrete
Low enough to be cool
Low enough to present
Low enough to be invisible

Their jean jackets envelope chests
Blanket stomachs and hide body frames
Ruptured from hard times on repeat
A China joint is headquarters
Beside headquarters
is a Yoga studio, Bike shop, and Pub
Here, they'll shoot the breeze
Deliberate on the worlds affairs
Whistle at School girls
Young enough to be their daughter's daughters
The panhandlers keep safe distance

Interruption is blasphemy
An accountant jogs pass
Unaware the generals are busy catering to
The salvation of this nation
Black Boys bump fist
Step around these fixtures
En route to Ascend class and break the backs
Of institutions built to kidnap them

Music from Bodegas drown out machinery that
Butchers history and the Kingdom of
6 generals who have weight of the universe
Suspended on slumped shoulders

Georgia Avenue

Jim crow's skeleton
fell out of
a police van
crashed onto the ashen pavement
paraded down Pennsylvania avenue
set fire to capitalism
brutalized the metal cavalry
of pigs
subsequently
announcing a %100 off sale
the city glowed
as Watts glowed
as Harlem glowed
as Ferguson glowed
for Freddie

Baltimore Power Keg

We are the pigmented grandbabies
of God whisperin sharecroppers
Stolen Daughters of the Galaxy
Bartered Sons of Gold Canyons
Summertime porch stories and fables
Melanin soaked Messiahs
Uninformed of their crowns
We breathe triumph and stroll
With burdened feet
Make rivers churn with our voices
Children of two choices
Die fighting or fight to die
Think deeply
O you son of Mansa
O you daughter of Nzinga
O you child of Ella
O you child of Malcolm
We are miles from Justice
Yet molecules from freedom
They will try to break you!
Do you hear me?!
They will try to break you
Time has been a comin
for reckoning
for sobering
for unshackling
for truth
for retribution
for liberation
for movement
for power, for power, for power, for power,
for power, for power, for power, for power.

Kingdoms Redemption

We cannot love without loss
Breathe without letting go
He who pays martyrdoms cost
Blooms in a winter's snow

Many Men have shape-shifted,
Just as the oak's leaves brown
Molested truth and missed it
Ignorance is renowned

Forgive them father

Born in the ghetto
more torn than geppetto
see these strings strapped seedlings
leave black mothers grieving
eyes damp as a meadow
our clocks never tick tocked
rulers never measured
nixon flooded us thick rocks
we stormed through that weather
whether the whether or nots
the song remains the same
pretty hard to get knowledge
while they're beating out our brains
no crystal stairs here
or either we're deranged
is it the buoyancy of hope?
or the soberness of pain ?
i watched a baby born addicted
ever since been conflicted
we never asked for this hell
now we struggle just to live well
hell, what your opinion?

Scribbles in the Concrete

Harriets song harriets song
i got a few runaways gettin carried along
sam cooke overlooked
but I never buried his palms
engineering a new nigga
new nigga
you knew nigga
niggas been down to long

now choose wisely
this pistol or freedom
a few tickets to serendipity
we couldn't redeem em'
this trail's been walked
our bodies been bought
keep quiet keep low
or it's all for naught

Keep Running

With eyes as calm as a Virginia pond in the fall

And cheek bones sitting high

Way too high

From smiling way too much

A little woman no taller than a 6th grader

Height upstaged by her 200lb heart

Hands with wrinkles that told the story of a perfectionist

Every bend in the skin paid homage

To a conquered obstacle she made submit to her will

My mother resided on earth

But was never really with us

Too pure for 100% of her soul to dwell here

In the land of fantasy, wretchedness and dreams

I still find myself jealous

Of the woman who by God's decree

I may never understand

Ummi

Beyond the 24 hour news cycle
There is a place
Where politicians eat the dreams of children
And men die for mineral wealth
Where Slavery is the order of the day
And peace is an ancient idea
Where men become obese from the flesh of Nations
And lies come bundled in tight-eyed smiles
Where disaster is a delicacy
And confusion is drank by the gallon

Where the puppet strings are made of iron ore
And dictatorship looks like salvation
Where life is auctioned to the highest bidder
And women hug boys they'll never see again
Where pleasure is constant misery
And poison sold wholesale

Where the righteous are made enemies
And enemies made righteous
And what you see is what's allowed
And what you know is what's been told
And what you hear is all their sound
And what you believe is a lie

And what you do is unplug
And what you do is unplug
And what you do is unplug

Yasiin

ABOUT THE AUTHOR

Tariq Touré is an Essayist, Poet and Community Advocate. A native Baltimorean, Touré is a former record holding, first team all state, all city athlete. Since the age of 19, Touré has professionally engaged in the development of at-risk African American Males of all ages in Baltimore and Washington D.C. Touré uses prose as a medium for shedding new light on issues such as social justice, racial inequality, Black culture and Black Muslim narratives. In addition, Touré's poetry has been featured in Baltimore's critically acclaimed 'City Paper Magazine'. In 2015 Touré was awarded with the Alumni Excellence award from his Alma Mater Bowie State University by the dept. of Social Work for social impact and community engagement. World renowned Hip Hop Artist 'Black Thought' has regarded Touré as the 'Amiri Baraka of our time' for his ability to speak truth to power though his penmanship.

PRAISE FOR BLACK SEEDS

⚘

"Tariq Toure is Baltimore's Black revolutionary voice. In the tradition of Amiri Baraka and James Baldwin, Toure masterfully uses his pen to attack white supremacy, expose systemic racism, and highlight the beauty that is the Black community. Toure doesn't hide behind his own articles, academia, social media or fake non-profit—no, Toure is one of the few real ones, he's in the street fighting for us, living what he pens and using a cocktail of activism and art to make the world a better place for all of us. Tariq Toure is our revolutionary voice and we are beyond proud of the way that he is representing us."

—D. Watkins, author of **The Beast Side: Living and Dying While Black in America**